Christ Among Us

The Diocese of Westminster explores the vision behind the challenges and opportunities of the future

A book offering material for:

✦ Daily Meditation
✦ Faith Sharing Sessions for Small Christian Communities
✦ Larger Parish Gatherings

Accompanied by the DVD, **Christ Among Us:** *Reflections by Cardinal Cormac Murphy-O'Connor*

Christ Among Us
INTRODUCTION

In Lent we are called to keep company with Christ. Through prayer, fasting and almsgiving the challenge is to enter into the desert with Christ and do what Christ did – to trust in the Father and consider what it is we are called to.

This Lent, following the publication of his White Paper on the future of the Diocese, our bishop, Cardinal Cormac Murphy-O'Connor, invites us to reflect on a particular dimension of our relationship with Christ, namely our relationship to his Church here in the Diocese of Westminster. What is it that the Lord has called me to do, here and now, in this place, in this community, in this local church?

In his White Paper, entitled *Communion and Mission: Pastoral Vision for the Diocese of Westminster,* the Cardinal outlines several themes; the Universal Call to Holiness; Small Christian Communities; Priesthood; the People of God and Lay Formation; Working Together in Mission. This booklet, *Christ Among Us*, is an opportunity to explore these themes alongside the Gospel readings given to us for Lent.

USING *CHRIST AMONG US* AS AN INDIVIDUAL

The daily meditations found in the following pages are offered for individual use. They are a response to the Scripture text and reflect on the season of Lent, but where appropriate the reflection and questions provided will help you as an individual to consider the themes given to us by the Cardinal.

We invite you to pray daily with these meditations. As God's own Word to us it will help us to enter into conversation with God.

Begin each week by reading the Bishop's Teaching and the Gospel reading for the Sunday with a question for reflection. We suggest that, as far as possible, you choose a regular time each day to use this booklet. Remind yourself as you begin that this is a special time for you to spend with God. Each day start by thanking God for this moment of prayer and ask him to help you to pray. Read through the Scripture passage, pause and then re-read it very slowly. See if the reflection helps to concentrate your thoughts. Stop to reflect and absorb any phrase or word that seems to stand out and speak to you. Use the questions for reflection to begin to direct your thoughts. Determine to carry these questions with you for the remainder the day.

Christ Among Us
INTRODUCTION

USING *CHRIST AMONG US* IN A SMALL CHRISTIAN COMMUNITY

For some of you these practical points are well known but for others they will be new. To new members of small communities we offer a big welcome. To everyone, please take time to read these few lines.

What will you be doing?

You will be **Gathering** as a small community to pray together and to share your life and faith. Take the time to get to know one another and meet in a reflective atmosphere with as few distractions as possible. It would be helpful to have a central focus, such as an open Bible, which would emphasise the central role of the Word.

The **Timing** of each session is important. Usually a session should last 90 minutes. Each session will have a balance of prayer, talking about your own experience, exploring Scripture, reflection, sharing and talking about how you are living your faith.

Prayer will take different forms and should be led by different people. Ordinarily, it is good to have about 15 minutes of prayer. Silence is an important part of the process. Do not be afraid to pause during your prayer time or, indeed, during the reflection for some quiet time.

Reflecting on **Experience** is essential to our spiritual lives. We need to reflect on *our story* – what we have experienced in our families, in our relationships and how it relates to the theme of the session and the teaching from the Bishop.

Then, we listen to **Scripture** – *God's story* – and we explore it, noticing what word, phrase or image from the Scripture speaks to us, what has touched our hearts. We are given some input to help us to **reflect** on what God is saying to us today. Each person who wants to talk is given the opportunity to do so. No one should dominate and no one should talk unless she or he wants to.

One of the essential gifts of faith sharing is how we take what we hear and live it out in our lives. Therefore, each week we have the opportunity to reflect on how *God's story* enlightens *our story* and invites us to **respond** – to renew our commitment to Christ. This is a time to look at how we are living Gospel values and to embrace new behaviours and attitudes.

Christ Among Us
INTRODUCTION

What is the leader of your group expected to do?

Each community will have its leader. A leader is not someone with all the answers who is there to put everybody else right. He or she is a fellow participant but with the particular responsibility of helping the community by:

- ◆ Preparing ahead of each session and developing a warm, accepting and open environment
- ◆ Guiding the group through each of the weekly sessions
- ◆ Sharing the various tasks among members of the group
- ◆ Listening and, when necessary, using the group session material to keep things on track
- ◆ Ensuring that every participant has the opportunity to speak if they wish. A silent contribution may have equal value

Your group leader and other members of your faith sharing community will encourage you to see the small community meeting not as a discussion group but as a sharing group through which it is hoped you will grow in faith. If you are a leader and have missed the training sessions, please talk to someone in your parish team about training.

Step 1 – Introductions and Opening Prayer

When you come together for the first time it will be important to introduce yourselves to each other. If possible it will also help to watch the *Cardinal's Call* on the *Christ Among Us* DVD (please ask your parish team if you do not have a copy of this). Thereafter, following the opening prayer, you will have an opportunity to catch-up with each other, but in particular to see how the previous week's session has influenced you in the meantime.

Step 2 – Our Bishop Teaches and Reflecting on our Experience

Begin by watching the relevant section of the *Christ Among Us* DVD or by reading aloud the extract from the Bishop's Teaching. Then you will be given the opportunity with the help of some questions to reflect upon and share something of your own experience. Additionally the DVD can be viewed at www.rcdow.org.uk.

Step 3 – Explore the Scriptures

Having listened to the Gospel for the week, reflect on what you have heard in a moment of silence. A further reflection is provided to help you explore the Scripture to which you have listened.

Christ Among Us
INTRODUCTION

Step 4 – Reflect
Having read or listened to the reflection provided, some questions are given to stimulate your own reflection. You will have the opportunity to share if you wish.

Step 5 – Respond and Closing Prayer
Finally, you are faced with the challenge of making a response that is roooted in Scriptures, guided by the Bishop's Teaching and which draws on your experience. How, in other words, am I to respond to what I have heard in this session? What difference will this make to me and how I witness to Christ?

USING *CHRIST AMONG US* IN A LARGE GROUP
The Group sessions for each week can be adapted easily for use by larger gatherings. You might be meeting as a large group and later break into smaller groups of 6-8 people. You might be meeting café style, sitting at tables of 6-8 people during the whole meeting. One way or the other, take the time to get to know one another and meet in a reflective atmosphere.

You will probably have a facilitator and the small groups might have a designated leader. Try to create a central focus, such as an open Bible which would emphasise the central role of the Word or a lighted candle.

The leader of the large group should follow the guidance and steps above to make the most of sharing the experience, the reflecting on scripture and the call to respond. The three periods of sharing will work best in smaller groups but Prayer, the reading of the Bishop's Teaching (or watching the DVD) and Scripture can all take place within the larger group.

What is the leader of your group expected to do?
Each meeting will have its facilitator but as with the small group meetings, each group will need a designated leader. This is not someone with all the answers. They are a fellow participants but with the particular responsibility of helping the group by:

✦ Preparing ahead of each session and being familiar with the material
✦ Guiding the group and using the book to keep the sharing on track

Communion and Mission
THE CARDINAL'S CALL

Jesus stood among them and said 'Peace be with you… as the Father sent me, I am sending you'.
John 20:19, 21

This promise and command of the Risen Christ has inspired the Church in every generation. Today Christ speaks these words with the same freshness. As the first Apostles heard this command, I, as an apostle today, am sent by the Lord to be Christ among you and to speak those same words: peace be with you.

What is this gift of peace I proclaim when I greet you at every Mass? It is the unifying presence of Christ among us. It is God's gift of his own Son. 'We may be certain, after such a gift that he will not refuse anything that he can give' (Romans 8:32). It is this promise that God will provide which gives me the confidence to call the local Church in Westminster to be the sign of hope to our world. Christ has given to us everything we need to be such a sign: in community; in word; in sacrament. My vision is to reanimate the local Church – our parishes, religious communities, families, schools, new movements, organisations, priests and people – to be the sign of God's presence in this place. We need to listen to what the Spirit is saying to our Diocese and together as one people recognise and embrace the mission which Christ has for us today. And what is this mission? It is to proclaim the boundless love that God has for his world.

I am aware we cannot be a sign of this love unless we deepen constantly our own love for God, for his Church and for one another. This is Christ's call to us – to grow in holiness by our dedication to prayer and the Liturgy, by our participation in community gathered around the Word of God, by recognising his unique call to each one of us, by living as the People of God working together. These are my priorities for the future. That we may grow together in our communion with one another and the Lord, and serve Christ in his mission.

+Cormac

Universal Call to Holiness
WEEK ONE

Our Bishop teaches

As Christians in any state or walk of life we are called to the fullness of Christian life and to the perfection of charity

Lumen Gentium, 40

It is the teaching of the Church that we are all called to holiness. This corresponds to the call to be perfect as our heavenly Father is perfect (Mt 5:48). In the pilgrimage towards perfection, the season of Lent helps us to turn away from sin and be faithful to the Gospel. This is a necessary part of our journey through the way of the Cross to the promise of future glory. Lent also reminds us that our thirst for holiness requires prayer which roots us in the Truth – sustaining us as we strive towards what Pope John Paul II called "a high standard of Christian living".

Our life of holiness, arising from our baptism, incorporates us into the body of Christ and the mystery of the Holy Trinity (*Catechism* 2014). Thus begins our 'divinisation' – a term dear to theologians of the Eastern Church – our sharing in the divine life through daily union with Christ.

The Eucharist is the ultimate source and nourishment of holiness, the greatest sacramental gift. In the Eucharist, we encounter and draw life from the Crucified, Risen and Glorified Christ. Pope Benedict, in Cologne, appealed to the young and to all believers to appreciate anew that the Eucharist is the Heart of Sunday (World Youth Day, Cologne, 21 August 2005).

The Year of the Eucharist, recently completed, was the culmination of the Eucharistic teaching and preaching of Pope John Paul II. He frequently called for a renewed reverence, a profound appreciation of the sacredness of the Eucharist, even a sense of amazement before the most holy and sanctifying Eucharist.

Universal Call to Holiness
WEEK ONE

First Sunday of Lent (5th March)
Mark 1: 12-15

*The Spirit drove him out into the wilderness
and he remained there for forty days, and was tempted by Satan.
He was with the wild beasts, and the angels looked after him.
After John had been arrested, Jesus went into Galilee.
There he proclaimed the Good News from God.
'The time has come' he said 'and the kingdom of God is close at hand.
Repent, and believe the Good News.'*

For your daily reflection

John the Baptist was an innocent victim. His only crime was preparing the way for Christ.

◆ Who have I condemned? Where have I misjudged?

*I love you Jesus, my love above all things.
I repent with my whole heart of having offended you.
Never permit me to separate myself from you again.
Grant that I may love you always and then do with me as you will.*

Universal Call to Holiness
WEEK ONE

Monday: Mark 1:15

The time has come

Christ's announcement that 'the time has come' is easily read in relation to his statement that the kingdom is close at hand. In the person of Christ, the kingdom had indeed arrived, for in Christ, God walked among us. However 'the time' that Christ speaks of in this passage is not simply a commentary on his presence and the arrival in him of the kingdom. Here 'the time' Christ speaks of is a time for choosing, a time of decision. The kingdom of God is close at hand. Are you for him or are you against him? Decide!

For your daily reflection

✦ Do I believe in God, the Father Almighty, Creator of heaven and earth?
✦ Do I believe in Jesus Christ, his only Son, our Lord, who was born of the Virgin Mary, was crucified, died and was buried, rose from the dead and is now seated at the right hand of the Father?
✦ Do I believe in the Holy Spirit, the holy catholic Church, the communion of saints, the forgiveness of sins, the resurrection of the body, and life everlasting?

*Christ with me, Christ before me,
   Christ behind me,
Christ in me, Christ beneath me,
   Christ above me,
Christ on my right, Christ on my left,
Christ when I lie down, Christ when I sit down,
   Christ when I arise,
Christ in the heart of everyone
   who thinks of me,
Christ in the mouth of everyone
   who speaks of me,
Christ in every eye that sees me,
Christ in every ear that hears me.*

from St Patrick's Breast Plate

Universal Call to Holiness
WEEK ONE

Tuesday: Mark 1:12

The spirit drove him out

At first sight this seems somewhat disturbing. How could the Spirit force anyone, force Christ, into doing anything? After all, force has no place in a loving relationship, let alone the relationship between the Father, the Son and the Holy Spirit, or God's relationship with us. We, it must be remembered, were given the freedom to love God or reject God. God does not force us to love him, that is a choice he gifted to us – a proof of his unsurpassable generosity. So, when the scripture speaks of the Spirit driving Christ out, the picture we have before us, is not of a Christ being pushed or forced into something, but of a passionate and driven Christ; a man on a mission, compelled from within by the same Holy Spirit that descended upon him at his baptism in the Jordan, and which was poured into us at our baptism.

For your daily reflection

✦ What mission am I passionate about and would like to embrace?
✦ How free do I feel in my relationship with God?
✦ Am I prepared to let God's power work in me?

Come Holy Spirit, fill the hearts of your faithful and enkindle in them the fire of your love.

Universal Call to Holiness
WEEK ONE

Wednesday: Mark 1:12

out into the wilderness

For the Jewish people, the desert was not somewhere that you went to escape, but a place where you went to encounter God. We cannot physically go into the desert; but Christ's wilderness experience, Christ's searching after God in a hostile environment, where temptation is all too alive can be a reality for us. Homelessness, illness, unemployment, old age, even youth – all these can be the wilderness where our search after God is keenest and our trust in him at its most tenuous.

For your daily reflection

- In prayer and the sacraments we encounter Christ. What part do these play in my life?
- Our need of God can be desperate when life can seem like one crisis after another, but what part does Christ play in my life when things are going well?

*Heavenly Father, make firm
    within me my efforts to be holy,
empty my heart of all needless anxiety,
and let me see that all things are passing.
In the heat of the day
    and the calm of the evening,
grant me the grace to seek
    and find you above all things,
to love and understand you
    more than anything.
Amen.*

*based on Thomas a Kempis,
The Imitation of Christ*

Universal Call to Holiness
WEEK ONE

Thursday: Mark 1:13

was tempted by Satan

Conscious as we are of Christ's divinity and perfection, it can be difficult to contemplate his being tempted. Of course Christ did not give in, but his being tempted was a reality. Moreover, we speak of a God who was generous enough to become truly human but, in explaining Christ's ability to resist temptation, we tend to take our fallen humanity – humanity as it has become and not as God intended it – as the blue-print for what it is to be truly human and, that done, to present the humanity which Christ assumed as something wholly extraordinary. 'Like us in all things but sin'. This is what we and countless generations have professed about Christ, and in professing it we must admit that Christ's refusal to give way to temptation was every bit as real and heroic as ours can be.

For your daily reflection

✦ Do I reject Satan?
✦ And all his works?
✦ And all his empty promises?

Saint Michael, Archangel, defend us in battle.
Be our protection against the wickedness and snares of the Devil.
May God rebuke him, we humbly pray;
and do thou, O Prince of the Heavenly Host,
by the power of God,
thrust into hell Satan
  and all the other evil spirits
who prowl about the world
  seeking the ruin of souls.
Amen.

Universal Call to Holiness
WEEK ONE

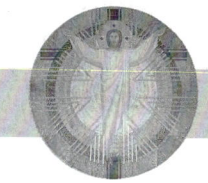

Friday: Mark 1:13

He was with the wild beasts and the angels looked after him.

Surrounded by wild beasts and the heat of the day Jesus could not have found the desert an hospitable place. For many people, honest self-reflection is not easy. Lent however is not a summons to do this by ourselves. Out in the wilderness, Christ was ministered to by the angels. His Father did not desert him. Put simply, Lent is not a journey, an obstacle course, to be travelled alone. Nor, for that matter, can it ever be an individual achievement; for whatever we achieve, we achieve through the graciousness of God.

For your daily reflection

✦ How conscious am I of God's goodness to me?

God our Father, in a wonderful way
   you guide our work and the work of angels.
May those who serve you constantly in heaven
   keep our lives safe from all harm on earth.
Grant this through our Lord Jesus Christ,
   your Son, who lives and reigns with you
   and the Holy Spirit.
Amen.
                        Adapted from the opening prayer
                              Feast of the Archangels

Universal Call to Holiness
WEEK ONE

Saturday: Mark 1:15

Repent, and believe the Good News

Lent is a time to admit to ourselves what it is that needs to be put right. Of course, the temptation is to think of the 'putting right' in purely physical terms: giving up smoking, drinking less, avoiding chocolate. Yet as laudable as all these are, and as beneficial as they may be to the body beautiful, doing Lent well involves a more fundamental question. It's not about stripping away that extra pound or dropping the unhealthy habits we have got into, rather it's an honest look at what has got in the way between us and God, between us and the Good News. In other words, Lent is an opportunity to consider our priorities.

For your daily reflection

- ✦ If God has figured in my past, where does he figure now and in the future?
- ✦ What is it that I have resolved to do or not do this Lent? Will it help me grow in my relationship with God?

Have mercy on me God in your kindness.
In your compassion, blot out my offence . . .
My offences truly I know them;
my sin is always before me . . .
indeed you love truth in the heart;
then in the secret of my heart teach
   me wisdom.
Amen.

Based on Psalm 50 (51)

Universal Call to Holiness
WEEK ONE — GROUP SESSION

You may want to watch the 'Cardinal's Call' on the *Christ Among Us* DVD to begin your group session. Alternatively, you may want to read the Cardinal's Call on page 7.

Opening Prayer

*Father, through our observance of Lent,
help us to understand the meaning
of your Son's death and resurrection,
and teach us to reflect it in our lives.*
                Opening Prayer, First Sunday of Lent

Listen to the Bishop's teaching for this week by watching the DVD or by reading the extract below.

The Eucharist is the ultimate source and nourishment of holiness, the greatest sacramental gift. In the Eucharist, we encounter and draw life from the Crucified, Risen and Glorified Christ. Pope Benedict, in Cologne, appealed to the young and to all believers to appreciate anew that the Eucharist is the Heart of Sunday (World Youth Day, Cologne, 21 August 2005).
                Extract from the Bishop's Teaching

Reflecting on our Experience

✦ What part does the Sunday Eucharist play in my life?

Explore the Scriptures

Mark 1:12-15

*The Spirit drove him out into the wilderness
    and he remained there for forty days
    and was tempted by Satan.
He was with the wild beasts,
    and the angels looked after him.
After John had been arrested
    Jesus went into Galilee.
There he proclaimed the Good News from God.
'The time has come' he said 'and the kingdom of
    God is close at hand.
Repent, and believe the Good News.'*

Both Matthew and Luke go into greater detail about Jesus' temptation in the desert. There in the face of Christ's hunger, isolation and powerlessness, Satan urges Christ to turn the dry stones into bread, to put God's faithfulness to the test, and to worship him rather than God in return for some absolute power. Obedient to the Father, and trusting in his love and fidelity, Christ chooses to be fed and sustained by his relationship with the Father. It is this relationship that fills the void created by his hungering and thirst.

For us the relationship which Christ has to his Father is something to aspire to. We, unlike Christ, have the habit of giving in to our temptations. Like Adam and Eve before us we erect barriers

Universal Call to Holiness

GROUP SESSION — WEEK ONE

between ourselves and God, choosing our own way rather than following his. Steeped as we tend to be in the knowledge of our own shortcomings, it would be all too easy to forsake the Christian living we are called to. However, despite our shortcomings, God has continuously expressed a willingness to be known. We sinned, we fell away from him and still he sent his Son whose triumph over sin opens up for us the way back to the Father and the prospect of everlasting life in union with Him.

In Christ, God issues us with an invitation to know him more fully. Yes, every time we celebrate the Eucharist we are given concrete proof of God's love for us, but in re-presenting Christ's sacrifice of himself on the Cross the Eucharist is also an invitation to explore the relationship between the Father and the Son. Here, as it were, as Calvary is set before us, the relationship between the Father and Son is displayed in all its mystifying intimacy and depth. More fully and finally, the Son, thirsting, isolated and powerless trusts in his Father and the Father, in raising Jesus from the dead, returns love for love.

In feasting on Christ's body and blood, we express the belief and hope that what nourished the relationship between the Father and the Son, will also transform our fumbling faithfulness into something more glorious.

Reflect

✦ Share something that strikes you from the Gospel reading.
✦ Jesus trusted in the Father to provide for all his needs. In the sacraments, Jesus promises that we will be fed, renewed, healed and sustained. Indeed it is often said that the Eucharist makes the Church. What does this mean for me?

Respond

This week – nourished by the Eucharist – how am I to embody the call to holiness?

Closing Prayer

*It were my soul's desire
to imitate my King.
It were my soul's desire
his ceaseless praise to sing.*

*It were my soul's desire
when heaven's gate is won
to find my soul's desire
clear shining like the sun.*

*Grant, Lord, my soul's desire
deep waves of cleansing sighs;
grant, Lord, my soul's desire
from earthly cares to rise.*

*This still my soul's desire
whatever life afford –
to gain my soul's desire
and see thy face, O Lord.*

Anonymous 11th Century

Small Christian Communities
WEEK TWO

Our Bishop teaches

In the sacred books the Father who is in heaven comes to meet his children with great love and speaks with them; there is such strength and power in the Word of God that it becomes the sustenance and energy of the Church, and for the Church's children it provides the strength of faith, the food of the soul and the pure and eternal source of spiritual life.

Dei Verbum, 21

In the Sacred Word, the Word of God, we receive the gift of Christ Himself. Moreover, as the Bishops of England, Wales and Scotland stated in the recent teaching document, *The Gift of Scripture,* the Scriptures, when read within the heart of the living Tradition of the community of faith, provide guidance on countless contemporary issues. The Word of God is for all of us and we are called not just to listen. We are empowered through our faith and the sacraments to proclaim the Word of God.

Throughout the Diocese many small communities have encouraged us and have helped us to share our faith based on the Sacred Scriptures. We pray together and we offer support to each other. In this atmosphere there arises among us a keen sense of mission to reach out to the world around us, proclaiming our conviction of faith in Christ Jesus.

Such is the high point of the gift of faith and the power of the Word of God that, nourished in our communion of faith, we reach out in mission, proclaiming Christ, the Saviour of the world. How wonderful is the Mission awaiting our Diocese as a *communion of communities*.

Small Christian Communities
WEEK TWO

Second Sunday of Lent (12th March)
Mark 9:2-10

*Jesus took with him Peter and James
and John and led them up a high mountain
where they could be alone by themselves.
There in their presence he was transfigured:
his clothes became dazzlingly white, whiter than
   any earthly bleacher could make them.
Elijah appeared to them with Moses; and they
   were talking with Jesus.
Then Peter spoke to Jesus: 'Rabbi,' he said 'it is
   wonderful for us to be here;
so let us make three tents, one for you, one for
   Moses and one for Elijah'.
He did not know what to say; they were
   so frightened.
And a cloud came, covering them in shadow; and
   there came a voice from the cloud,
'This is my Son, the Beloved. Listen to him.'
Then suddenly, when they looked round,
 they saw no one with them any more but
   only Jesus.
As they came down from the mountain he
   warned them to tell no one what they had
   seen, until after the Son of Man had risen from
   the dead.
They observed the warning faithfully,
   though among themselves they discussed what
   'rising from the dead' could mean.*

For your daily reflection

✦ What does 'rising from the dead' mean for me?

*Glory be to the Father
and to the Son and to the Holy Spirit,
as it was in the beginning,
is now and ever shall be,
world without end.
Amen.*

Small Christian Communities
WEEK TWO

Monday: Mark 9:2-3

*Jesus took with him Peter and James and John, and led them up a high mountain where they could be alone, by themselves.
There in their presence he was transfigured: his clothes became dazzlingly white, whiter than any earthly bleacher could make them.*

Mark doesn't actually say why Jesus brought the disciples up the mountain; but we remember the fact that Jesus withdrew to be with the Father at the decisive moments in his life. On this occasion, Jesus invites three disciples to be with him. This invitation is something Jesus issues to us again and again if we are willing to be led. We know that mountains are places where divine revelations occur at various places in Scripture and this mountain was another place of meeting – the meeting of the Old and New Testament. What occurs is something extraordinary. Jesus' transformation gives us a glimpse of the manner in which he reveals himself in the Eucharist. The glorified Christ the disciples met on the mountain is the same Christ we encounter in the Eucharist. They have entered into a mystery; the experience has been overwhelming; there are unanswered questions.

For your daily reflection

◆ Jesus invites us to the mountain. Am I willing to be led?
◆ Can I name those times when I have met God?

Father, help us to remember to pray at the decisive moments in our lives. Transform us as you transform the bread and wine into the body and blood of Christ. Amen.

Small Christian Communities
WEEK TWO

Tuesday: Mark 9:4

Elijah appeared to them with Moses; and they were talking with Jesus.

Moses the law giver and Elijah the prophet both suffered because of their fidelity to God – Jesus, too, would suffer. Their presence on this mountain points to Jesus' role in fulfilling God's promises made in the Old Testament. Moreover it stands in stark contrast to the hill of Golgotha where he kept company with criminals. On the holy mountain, Jesus' clothing becomes dazzlingly bright; on the hill at Golgotha, his clothing will be torn from his body.

For your daily reflection

✦ Imagine Peter and his companions' feelings that Jesus was the Messiah that all generations had been waiting for. We look to Christ's second coming. If it were today how would I feel?

My heart has prompted me to seek your face; I seek it, Lord; so do not hide from me.
Entrance Antiphon
Second Sunday of Lent

Small Christian Communities
WEEK TWO

Wednesday: Mark 9:5-6

Then Peter spoke to Jesus: "Rabbi, he said, it is wonderful for us to be here; so let us make three tents, one for you, one for Moses, and one for Elijah." He did not know what to say; they were so frightened.

Quite naturally, the disciples want to make sense of this happening. Peter wanted to prolong the experience of Jesus' transfiguration by building temporary dwellings for Moses, Elijah and Christ. The tent had important Old Testament connotations. The theme of tenting is found in Exodus (25:8-9) where Israel is told to make a tent (or a tabernacle) so that God can dwell among his people – living as his people were living.

In the face of what was happening, Peter's understanding was inadequate. At the end of this Gospel passage we find him discussing these events with his companions. We too are reliant on the wisdom and understanding of others. Part of the challenge of this Lent for us is to reflect on how our understanding can be deepened by sharing.

For your daily reflection

✦ Have I ever had an experience where such a revelation has dawned on me?
✦ Do I feel safe to encounter Christ outside the tabernacle?

Jesus, you always welcome me into your presence;
but there are times when I do not even notice that you are there.
Help me always to be aware of your presence and your love in my life.
Amen.

Small Christian Communities
WEEK TWO

Thursday: Mark 9:7

And a cloud came, covering them in shadow; and there came a voice from the cloud,
"This is my Son, the Beloved; listen to him!"

The voice from the cloud is a divine voice, *"This is my Son, the Beloved"*. As such, the cloud is a symbol of life and hope. God was assumed to be the author of life and the ground of hope. In Exodus (40:34-38), a cloud covered the tent of meeting, which was filled with the glory of the Lord. The cloud symbolism and the reference to Jesus as *'my beloved Son'* indicate that the speaker is God, who tells us to listen to Jesus – revealer of God. God is revealed to us in the Word of God, in the Church's liturgy and in gathering around Scripture together in community.

For your daily reflection

- ✦ How and where do I listen to God speaking to me in the Scriptures?
- ✦ God said, "This is my Son, the Beloved". Do I hear, feel God calling me 'beloved'?

Father,
Reveal yourself to us as we gather in prayer
*   and as you speak to us in Scripture.*
We ask this through Christ our Lord.
Amen.

Small Christian Communities
WEEK TWO

Friday: Mark 9:8

Then suddenly, when they looked round, they saw no one with them any more, but only Jesus.

Suddenly Jesus stands alone with them as his *ordinary* self. The experience has ended abruptly. It was a preview; but before Jesus' glory can be revealed to the world, he must return to his every-day life and make his way to Jerusalem. We sometimes have experiences of God; once they are over, we take them back to our *ordinary* life transformed by the experience. Life is never the same again. Once we have had a real or dramatic experience of God, the challenge is to see the extraordinary grace of God at work in ordinary things.

For your daily reflection

✦ St. Theresa of Lisieux talked about doing the ordinary things extraordinarily well. How do I integrate my experiences of God into my every-day life?

Jesus, today I will see you in the people I meet – in the ordinary experiences of my life.
Transform me into the person you want me to become.
Amen.

Small Christian Communities
WEEK TWO

Saturday: Mark 9:9-10

As they came down the mountain, he warned them to tell no one what they had seen, until after the Son of Man had risen from the dead.
They observed the warning faithfully, though among themselves they discussed what 'rising from the dead' could mean.

We can be certain in the aftermath of the transfiguration that these apostles had seen Christ in a way that no-one else had ever seen him before. Yet Jesus warned them to tell no-one about what they had seen. Why? A possible explanation of Christ's caution is his own awareness that there was more to be accomplished. At that moment, the apostles were being asked not to speak about it because they did not have the complete story. It was a picture that would only be complete after the passion, death and resurrection.

For your daily reflection

✦ Revelation is a life-long experience which the disciples explored together. With whom do I explore God's revelation?

Father, complete in me Jesus' revelation of your love.
Lead me, guide me and mould me in your ways, O Lord.
Amen.

Small Christian Communities
WEEK TWO — GROUP SESSION

Opening Prayer

Let us pray in this season of Lent for the gift of integrity.
Father of light, in you is found no shadow of change but only the fullness of life and limitless truth.
Open our hearts to the voice of your Word and free us from the original darkness that shadows our vision.
Restore our sight that we may look upon your Son who calls us to repentance and a change of heart, for he lives and reigns with you for ever and ever.
Amen.

Opening Prayer
Second Sunday of Lent

Listen to the Bishop's teaching for this week by watching the DVD or by reading the extract below.

Throughout the Diocese many small communities have encouraged us and have helped us to share our faith based on the Sacred Scriptures. We pray together and we offer support to each other. In this atmosphere there arises among us a keen sense of mission to reach out to the world around us, proclaiming our conviction of faith in Christ Jesus. Such is the high point of the gift of faith and the power of the Word of God, that nourished in our communion of faith, we reach out in mission, proclaiming Christ, the Saviour of the world. How wonderful is the Mission awaiting our Diocese as a *communion of communities*.

Extract from the Bishop's teaching

Reflecting on our Experience

- ✦ What experience do I have of small communities?
- ✦ How might a small community gathered around the Scriptures strengthen the life of my parish and give me a sense of belonging?

Explore the Scriptures

Mark 9:2-10

Jesus took with him Peter and James and John and led them up a high mountain where they could be alone by themselves. There in their presence he was transfigured: his clothes became dazzlingly white, whiter than any earthly bleacher could make them.

Small Christian Communities
GROUP SESSION — WEEK TWO

Elijah appeared to them with Moses; and they were talking with Jesus.
Then Peter spoke to Jesus: 'Rabbi,' he said 'it is wonderful for us to be here; so let us make three tents, one for you, one for Moses and one for Elijah'.
He did not know what to say; they were so frightened.
And a cloud came, covering them in shadow; and there came a voice from the cloud,
'This is my Son, the Beloved. Listen to him.'
Then suddenly, when they looked round, they saw no one with them any more but only Jesus.
As they came down from the mountain he warned them to tell no one what they had seen, until after the Son of Man had risen from the dead.
They observed the warning faithfully, though among themselves they discussed what 'rising from the dead' could mean.

We talk about the Trinity as a communion of love and as such Father, Son and Holy Spirit may be seen as the icon for all *small communities*. The Apostles, led by Jesus, were the first small Christian community. They met frequently, prayed together, studied scriptures together, and shared their experiences together.

Jesus took three of them to the mountain to pray; curiously, the same three men were closest to him in the Garden of Gethsemane. As well as being with him for this experience of light on the mountain top, they were also present with him in one of his darkest moments. Christ is at the centre of these experiences. The disciples come down from the mountain into the valley having experienced this intimacy with our Lord.

It is possible for us to climb the mountain in order to pause, to contemplate and to be immersed in the mystery of God's light. Mount Tabor represents all the mountains that lead us to God; we are invited to make the ascent to the mountain and to the light. In these experiences and in our darkest moments, we are invited to listen to what God is saying to us. Seeing and hearing and contemplating are ways that lead us there – to a place where God is revealed to us. Some find this mountain experience we are speaking of in their small Christian communities; like the disciples, we also meet Jesus in the reality of our daily lives. In our small Christian communities, we pray together, we listen to the scriptures together and we share experiences together – we meet Jesus as we gather and we are transfigured.

Small Christian Communities
WEEK TWO — GROUP SESSION

What are transfigured men and women like? As the late Pope John Paul II said, "The answer is very beautiful: they are people who follow Christ in living and dying; they are people who are inspired by him and who let themselves be imbued with the grace that he gives us" (Homily, 11 March 2001). We become open to the gradual transformation of our attitudes into his attitudes – the beatitudes – so that we can discern how God is calling us to achieve the Kingdom. This Kingdom is not *our thing* and we often have to give up our own ideas about how to achieve it – as Peter had to be led by Jesus to do. To be at the service of the Kingdom, we must accept the unexpected of the person of Jesus as he presents himself to us through the Church today.

Reflect

- Share something that strikes you from the Gospel reading.
- How can the sharing of my faith with others deepen my understanding?
- Do I understand myself as a revealer of God to others?
- Peter said, "Lord, it is wonderful for us to be here." Will I say that as I leave this gathering?

Respond

- How can your parish continue to develop as a community of communities? Contact the *Pastoral Renewal Support Team* for help in supporting Small Christian Communities (020 7931 6064).
- What are the strengths and riches in your parish community that you want to celebrate? During the weekend of July 14th-16th 2006 every parish is invited to celebrate its life of faith and mission by taking part in the *Open the Doors* festival. How can your parish participate? Contact the Parish Events Coordinator for more details (020 7931 6064).

Closing Prayer

Heavenly Father, transfigure us into men and women who are more like you.
Fill our community with the light of your love and change our hearts so that we are willing to be led to the mountains and to follow you into the valleys as well.
We trust in your wisdom and care, and praise your Holy Name.
Help us to see only you, Lord, and to be witnesses to the light.
In Jesus' name we pray. Amen.

Priesthood
WEEK THREE

Our Bishop teaches

Christ, high priest and unique mediator, has made of the Church 'a kingdom, priests for his God and father.'

Catechism 1546

Discussion of vocations gives rise to disappointment and even hints of pessimism in many quarters because of the decline in the number of vocations compared to a few decades ago. Here we must be careful not to be defeatist. There is reason for hope and this is especially true of our own Diocese of Westminster this year. There is indeed a need to recover an attitude of active enthusiasm to allow the work of promoting vocations to flourish. With this in mind, in the *White Paper*, I call for a 'stronger culture of vocations.' Aside from concern about the quantity of vocations, positive commitment in faith, from all of us, will support and enhance the quality of response.

Christ's Priesthood challenges us to understand that there is a complementarity between the priesthood of the laity and the ministerial priesthood. There is a mutual nourishment between the lived vocation of the lay faithful and that of the ordained priest. On this point the teaching of the Catechism of the Catholic Church is worthy of recall: "Christ, high priest and unique mediator, has made of the Church 'a kingdom, priests for his God and father.' The whole community of believers is, as such, priestly. While the common priesthood of the faithful is exercised by the unfolding of baptismal grace – a life of faith, hope and charity, a life according to the Spirit, – the ministerial priesthood is at the service of the common priesthood. It is directed at the unfolding of the baptismal grace of all Christians" (*Catechism* 1546/7).

Priesthood
WEEK THREE

Third Sunday of Lent (19th March)
John 2:13-25

Just before the Jewish Passover Jesus went up to Jerusalem, and in the Temple he found people selling cattle and sheep and pigeons, and the money changers sitting at their counters there.

Making a whip out of some cord, he drove them all out of the Temple, cattle and sheep as well, scattered the money changers' coins, knocked their tables over and said to the pigeon-sellers, 'Take all this out of here and stop turning my Father's house into a market'.

Then his disciples remembered the words of scripture: Zeal for your house will devour me.

The Jews intervened and said, 'What sign can you show us to justify what you have done?'

Jesus answered, 'Destroy this sanctuary, and in three days I will raise it up'.

The Jews replied, 'It has taken forty-six years to build this sanctuary: are you going to raise it up in three days?'

But he was speaking of the sanctuary that was his body, and when Jesus rose from the dead, his disciples remembered that he had said this, and they believed the scripture and the words he had said.

During his stay in Jerusalem for the Passover many believed in his name when they saw the signs that he gave, but Jesus knew them all and did not trust himself to them; he never needed evidence about any man; he could tell what a man had in him.

For your daily reflection

✦ Do I expect signs from God to strengthen my faith? If so, what would they be?

Receive the Gospel of Christ
whose herald you now are.
Believe what you read,
teach what you believe,
and practice what you teach.
                      Rite of the Ordination of Deacons

Priesthood
WEEK THREE

Monday: John 2:16

Take all this out of here and stop turning my Father's house into a market.

Our initial reaction to this text is often of surprise and even shock, that our Lord would show such harshness. Anger of course is a natural emotion but left unchecked it can become a deadly sin. We know that Christ, who is like us in all things but sin, must therefore be showing a righteous anger. It is a reaction motivated by love and not merely hate of something which is clearly wrong. We each have the ability to do this and so share in Christ's priesthood; an innate desire to uphold and protect all that is sacred. The virtue of religion is something we ought to foster and nourish during Lent, as we seek to draw from the liturgy and our places of worship a deeper awareness of Christ. The beauty we can experience in our churches will enlighten us to see that which disfigures humanity and have the courage to challenge it. Just as Jesus saw the need to rid the Temple of clutter, so too can we rid ourselves of whatever it is that prevents us from being pure for God at Easter.

For your daily reflection

✦ Do I take the opportunities God gives to me to challenge what is evil and defend what is holy?

God our Father, in your infinite love and goodness you have shown us that prayer, fasting and almsgiving are remedies for sin. Accept the humble admission of our guilt, and when our conscience weighs us down let your unfailing mercy raise us up.
We make our prayer through Christ our Lord. Amen.

Divine Office
Morning Prayer of Third Sunday in Lent

Priesthood
WEEK THREE

Tuesday: John 2:17

Zeal for your house will devour me

The disciples' recollection of Psalm 69 was enough to remind them of the centrality of the Temple as a house of prayer. Our churches are no less important for us as the place for our encounter with the living God. Reverence and devotion is of the utmost importance if we are to preserve as well as restore peace and tranquility for our souls. We cannot do that if we fail to make any meaningful distinction between our conduct outside the building and the self-composure necessary to instil quiet and silence where we can hear God speak to us. Each of us on entering the church is seeking to draw close to God in prayer and praise. We best achieve this by respecting that others seek it too, fostering whatever we can to be disposed to inner tranquility, including a patient understanding for parents of little ones who also seek to encounter God in a spirit of prayer. Where conversation and non-liturgical activity in church is legitimate, let it be restrained and respectful for the sake of others out of generous and disciplined love. In this way we will be uniting ourselves with the ministry of the priest to lead others to Christ.

For your daily reflection

✦ Are there ways in which I might embrace the time of prayer in church with more devotion and consideration for others?
✦ What can I do to lessen the anxiety of parents and carers who have difficulty to sustain the concentration of their families at Mass?

One of the things that keeps us at a distance from perfection is, without doubt, our tongue.
For when one has gone so far as to commit no faults in speaking, the Holy Spirit assures us that we are perfect.
And since the worst way of speaking is to speak too much, speak little and well, little and gently, little and simply, little and charitably, little and amiably.

St Francis de Sales
A year with the Saints

Priesthood
WEEK THREE

Wednesday: John 2:21

But he was speaking of the sanctuary that was his body

Hindsight is a wonderful gift. The glaring truth often only dawns on us when we look back on events in the light of our experience now. The same is true for the disciples on recalling Christ's words at seeing him risen from the dead. Our bodies too are temples, sanctuaries of the same Holy Spirit. They don't belong to us in the same way that we might consider other things do, like a commodity to be used as the whim might take us. It is precisely because my body and soul has been purchased at the highest price, the Precious Blood of Christ, that I must also be a victim like him, offering all I have as daily service to his glory. Through all the physical experiences of our lives we recognise that our bodies are God's amazing gift to us for him and as such deserve our single-minded respect, care, nourishment and moral integrity.

For your daily reflection

✦ How can I be more appreciative of the presence of the Spirit in my body and in the bodies of others?

Look with favour on your family, Lord
   and as at this time we restrain the desires
   of the body may our hearts burn with
   love of you.
We make our prayer through Christ our Lord.
Amen.

Divine Office, Morning Prayer
Tuesday Week Three of Lent

Priesthood
WEEK THREE

Thursday: John 2:22

they believed the scripture and the words he had said

The liturgy of the Word is a fundamental element of our praying the Mass. We must be equally attentive to the Word that is proclaimed and spoken as we desire to be attentive toward the Real Presence of the Lord in the Bread that is blessed and broken. The priest is entrusted with the enormous privilege and urgent task to preach the Word of God in season and out of season. That is to say, to preach the truth of Christ through the teaching of the Church even when that truth is not always welcome. By the grace of ordination priests have an obligation and capacity to perform this ministry with generosity and zeal. As such, the lay faithful must equally support them with their prayers and attentiveness, that the priests' gifts for the ministry of the Word may flourish, uplift hearts and inspire a true communion of persons. Then having received the Word, the lay faithful are entrusted to bring it to others.

For your daily reflection

✦ Do I proclaim God's Word through these spiritual works of mercy? Instructing, advising, consoling, comforting, as well as forgiving and bearing wrongs patiently. (*Catechism* 2447)

O my God come to me so that you may dwell in me and I may dwell in you.
　　　　St. John Vianney, Patron of Parish Clergy

Priesthood
WEEK THREE

Friday: John 2:23

many believed in his name when they saw the signs that he gave

The stark contrast between Christ's popularity on entering Jerusalem with his degradation on the cross reminds us that we must guard against anything that might appear shallow in our relationship with the Lord. We live in a world that is saturated with images, sounds and sights heightened through mind-blowing technology and speed. We have to remember that our communication with God is not on a remote-control button but is often borne out of enduring love and patient hope.

Through ever deeper prayer, cherishing family and friends and listening to the teaching of the Church we gain the wisdom of Christ. Let us resist the clamour of the world around us which insists on putting God to the test. The sacraments are outward signs of inward grace. Let us rejoice in that loving presence of God and resist an exaggerated desire for material things which are mere outward signs of inward space.

For your daily reflection

✦ How can I exercise a greater detachment from material possessions and appreciate the signs of God's love in simple things?

Let nothing disturb you
   nothing frighten you.
All things are passing;
   patient endurance attains all things:
   one whom God possesses wants nothing
   for God alone suffices.
                    Bookmark of St. Teresa of Avila

Priesthood
WEEK THREE

Saturday: John 2:24-25

Jesus knew them all and did not trust himself to them; he never needed evidence about any man; he could tell what a man had in him.

Saturday is often the day in the parish for the celebration of penance and reconciliation. Priests are entrusted to be ready and available to receive repentant sinners and restore them to hope and grace in Christ. It is a truly joyful sacrament! The power to read souls (to perceive the hidden reality of a person) is a charism that our Lord displayed with remarkable tenderness and compassion. Such a gift and power to absolve and forgive resides in priestly ministry. A priest whose heart and spirit burns with love for people can often benefit from being very perceptive and understanding of what most concerns the hearts of those in his care. In our love and support and appreciation of pastors, let us pray that the Church is truly enriched with an abundance of this gift in the priesthood, so that we in turn can approach them with confidence to ask for God's mercy.

Let us never be afraid to ask our priests for God's help and may they be emboldened anew with the same thirst for souls that Christ expressed on the Cross.

For your daily reflection

✦ How can I deepen my appreciation of God's abundant love for me in the sacrament of reconciliation?

May the Passion of our Lord Jesus Christ, the merits of the Blessed Virgin Mary and of all the Saints, whatever good I do, whatever evil I suffer, gain for me a remission of sins, an increase in grace and the reward of everlasting life.

Adaptation of priest's thanksgiving prayer after absolution.

Priesthood
WEEK THREE GROUP SESSION

Opening Prayer

Let us learn . . . to live a contagious and communicative faith, because a "harmless" faith that does not say anything to anyone, that is not witnessed to, remains a "wasted" gift.

Homily of Pope Benedict at the Mass of Beatification of Charles de Foucauld 13 November 2005

Listen to the Bishop's teaching for this week by watching the DVD or by reading the extract below.

Christ's Priesthood challenges us to understand that there is a complementarity between the priesthood of the laity and the ministerial priesthood. There is a mutual nourishment between the lived vocation of the lay faithful and that of the ordained priest.

Extract from Bishop's teaching

Reflecting on our Experience

- What is my reaction to someone who says they are going to get married?
- What is my reaction to someone who says they have chosen to be single?
- What is my reaction to someone who expresses a desire to become a priest or to enter the religious life?

Explore the Scriptures

John 2:13-25

Just before the Jewish Passover Jesus went up to Jerusalem, and in the Temple he found people selling cattle and sheep and pigeons, and the money changers sitting at their counters there. Making a whip out of some cord, he drove them all out of the Temple, cattle and sheep as well, scattered the money changers' coins, knocked their tables over and said to the pigeon-sellers, 'Take all this out of here and stop turning my Father's house into a market'.
Then his disciples remembered the words of scripture: Zeal for your house will devour me.
The Jews intervened and said, 'What sign can you show us to justify what you have done?'
Jesus answered, 'Destroy this sanctuary, and in three days I will raise it up'.
The Jews replied, 'It has taken forty-six years to build this sanctuary: are you going to raise it up in three days?'
But he was speaking of the sanctuary that was his body, and when Jesus rose from the dead, his disciples remembered that he had said this, and they believed the scripture and the words he had said.
During his stay in Jerusalem for the Passover many believed in his name when they saw the signs that he gave, but Jesus knew them all and

GROUP SESSION WEEK THREE

Priesthood

did not trust himself to them; he never needed evidence about any man; he could tell what a man had in him.

No doubt we have all heard of "tough love." Any parent would be able to relate to the reality of having to discipline a child out of love so that they might grow in obedience and respect. God as our loving Father knows too well how disobedient our hearts can be towards his will. As we reflect upon this dramatic scene in the life of our Lord, we come to a new awareness of how sometimes God's grace can be savage in its effect in our lives.

During this week we reflect on the role and responsibility of the ordained priesthood and how the lay faithful sustain and support that role by their living fully the royal priesthood which they share through baptism. Every priest through his personality, his gifts, talents and strengths reflects some of the many facets of Jesus' own high priesthood.

So too in our Lord's cleansing of the Temple, we witness an icon of what must be an element of priestly love and service today. Just like Christ, the priest must challenge, confront, admonish, instruct, as well as console, comfort and placate. Like any personality, there must be a balance of all these traits so that people experience a consistent image of a man conformed to the likeness of the Lord.

The Lord must have been deeply hurt at the level of disrespect which had been allowed to corrupt the sacred precincts. His cleansing of the Temple then is a perfectly understandable, legitimate and expected action of his own priestly ministry. If Christ were to stand amidst the scandals and sacrileges of our day, not least society's unwillingness to preserve the sacredness of all human life, would his anger not equally be felt?

And yet the truth is, that in the midst of moral bankruptcy, he waits to speak out in protest against all evil, corruption and injustice through *our* voice and the courage of *our* witness. And this prophetic voice of challenge, the wake-up call to all that is corrupt, distorted and anti-life around us must be heard loudest among our priests. They, in turn, will be sustained with courage in this leadership by the real support, encouragement and affirmation offered by the people. To be a priest in today's world is not an easy calling and our inspiration and appreciation of the priest must stem from believing in the risen, glorified body of Christ still bearing the marks of his passion and death.

The marks of suffering, the beautiful wounds of love, borne in patience and hope and courage are the *icon* of the dignity of the priesthood. As we journey through this season to know and experience the joy of the Risen Christ, may it be

Priesthood
WEEK THREE   GROUP SESSION

that conviction which will make all of us, like the Apostles and in union with our priests, bold in our Christian witness.

People with zeal for God's house, the Church, unafraid to witness to truth, courageous enough to speak out against injustice and confident in declaring that the Gospel of life will be victorious over the culture of death!

Reflect

- Share something that strikes you from the Gospel reading.
- Do I knowingly avoid opportunities to witness in front of others to the truth of Catholic teaching on life and holiness?
- How could I become better informed about what the Church teaches on matters of faith and morals?
- What might I do to give someone hope and encouragement when they have doubts, fears and anxieties?

Respond

Saturday March 25th is the Feast of the Annunciation. Why not organise a day of Eucharistic adoration or a holy hour in the parish including the Pope's intentions to restore a culture of life?

Organise a promotional event for vocations and prayers for the Priesthood. Contact Fr Chris Vipers, for help and assistance (020 7798 9083); *www.rcdow.org.uk/vocations*.

Try to find out more about the *Alive and Kicking* campaign to alert society to the sacredness of human life from conception to death and see how your parish could become involved (020 7584 7186); *www.aliveandkickingcampaign.org*.

Closing Prayer

O Mary, grant that all who believe in your Son may proclaim the Gospel of life with honesty and love to the people of our time.
Obtain for them the grace to accept that Gospel as a gift ever new, the joy of celebrating it with gratitude throughout their lives and the courage to bear witness to it resolutely, in order to build, together with all people of good will, the civilisation of truth and love, to the praise and glory of God, the Creator and lover of life.

Evangelium Vitae, John Paul II, 1995

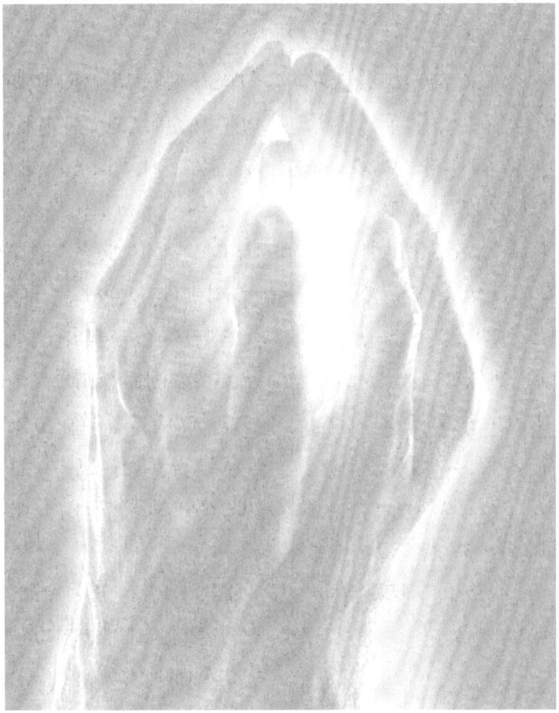

People of God and Lay Formation
WEEK FOUR

Our Bishop teaches

But you are a chosen race, a royal priesthood, a consecrated nation, a people set apart to sing the praises of God who called you out of the darkness into his wonderful light

1 Peter 2:9

We are part of a society that has lost touch with its religious narrative and lost confidence in its traditions of faith. We are an indifferent society more than a hostile one. If we are to witness to Christ and his resurrection, we need to be deeply grounded in our life of faith. In order to evangelise we ourselves must be evangelised. This is the *new evangelisation* that the Church in its teaching repeatedly calls us all to. If we are to speak about God we must have a renewed contact with God and his loving call to justice and mercy.

I believe that if we work together, we can all be helped to find our particular missionary calling. At the heart of that calling is a need to respond to the deep-seated yearning which each person has for God. Indeed, this is the duty given to us in the writing of the Second Vatican Council in the Document *Gaudium et Spes* where we are invited to respond to the joy and the hope the grief and the anguish of the men and women of our time.

This necessarily involves the promotion of the vocation and mission of lay people. We are the body of Christ, his hands in the world today.

In the course of his ministry, John Paul II continuously reminded us of the importance of the lay apostolate. In the final year of his life, dedicated to the Eucharist, he reminded us that that apostolate and the effectiveness of this mission is rooted in the strength which only the Eucharist can provide.

With such an awareness the faithful of Westminster could take to heart the exhortation of St Peter: "But you are a chosen race, a royal priesthood, a consecrated nation, a people set apart to sing the praises of God who called you out of the darkness into his wonderful light" (1 Peter 2:9).

People of God and Lay Formation
WEEK FOUR

Fourth Sunday of Lent (26th March)
John 3:14-21

Jesus said to Nicodemus:

'The Son of Man must be lifted up as Moses lifted up the serpent in the desert, so that everyone who believes may have eternal life in him.
Yes, God loved the world so much that he gave his only Son, so that everyone who believes in him may not be lost but may have eternal life.
For God sent his Son into the world not to condemn the world, but so that through him the world might be saved.
No one who believes in him will be condemned; but whoever refuses to believe is condemned already, because he has refused to believe in the name of God's only Son.
On these grounds is sentence pronounced: that though the light has come into the world men have shown they prefer darkness to the light because their deeds were evil.
And indeed, everybody who does wrong hates the light and avoids it, for fear his actions should be exposed; but the man who lives by the truth comes out into the light, so that it may be plainly seen that what he does is done in God.'

For your daily reflection

✦ Created in the image of God, we are called to imitate his generosity. What am I generous with?
✦ What limitations are there to my generosity? Where do I draw the line?

Dearest Lord, teach me to be generous.
teach me to serve you as you deserve;
to give and not to count the cost;
to fight, and not to heed the wounds;
to labour, and not to seek to rest;
to give of myself and not to ask for reward,
except the reward of knowing
that I am doing your will.
St. Ignatius of Loyola

People of God and Lay Formation
WEEK FOUR

Monday: John 3:15

That everyone who believes may have eternal life in him

St Augustine prayed "Give me chastity and continence, but not yet!" Putting things off is the human way. For many, things eternal are about the future. The Christ of John's Gospel directs us to think in a different way. For John the Eternal Life that Christ freely offers ought to be experienced now so that it can be fully revealed in the future. This sounds contradictory – that we can have eternity now and enjoy it fully in the future – but it is not. Isn't that what we know about the Mass? It is both a foretaste and a promise of heaven. For us, living the eternal way is the way to eternity. We received the call to living that way at baptism when the seed of eternal life was awakened in us. Knowing that this gift is ours has challenging consequences. To live in the hope and reality of eternity means allowing the Lord to transform us – to transform how we think and act. It means seeing things through the eyes of the Eternal One. It means recognising that through the faith given to me in baptism, we have a duty to reflect eternity and its values in our lives.

For your daily reflection

✦ Eternal Life has to be lived now. In what ways is this a challenge for me?

My Lord and my God, thank you
  for drawing me to yourself.
Make me desire more deeply
  that knowledge of you which is eternal life.
                                Margaret Dewey

People of God and Lay Formation
WEEK FOUR

Tuesday: John 3:16

God loved the world so much that he gave his only Son

This biblical phrase is much loved. For some Christians it is quoted like a mantra. Yet its familiarity can make us forget its radical message. God chose to love the world. St John sees the "world" not as a physical object but, as one commentator put it, rather as "the whole of humanity apart from, yet loved by, God." Despite our sinfulness, God, the loving Father, chose to love us and to give us the freedom to choose whether to give that love in return. Every parent, anyone who has been in love knows how risky this kind of love is. The baptised community of the Church are those who recognise and live in the love of God. Yet the startling message of today is that the love which God shows in sending his Son is a love not just for the saved, not just for the religious. God chose to love *all* humanity because, as Genesis reminds us, "God saw *all* that he had made and it was very good". Christ's coming assures us that God still loves the whole of humanity (warts and all!) with intensity and passion. Christ's crucifixion which we shall soon commemorate is not a gift for Christians alone. It is an eternal act of love for all. In declaring his love for all humanity, Christ challenges the community of the baptised to be a community of love for the sake of the whole world.

For your daily reflection

✦ In the early days people said of the Church "See how these Christians love one another". Could that be said of my parish?
✦ How is that love manifested in the wider community?

God our Father, in obedience to you your only Son accepted death on the Cross for the salvation of mankind.
We acknowledge the mystery of the Cross on earth.
May we receive the gift of redemption in heaven.
We ask this through our Lord Jesus Christ, your Son, who lives and reigns with you and the Holy Spirit, one God, for ever and ever. Amen.

Opening prayer, feast of the Exaltation of the Holy Cross

People of God and Lay Formation
WEEK FOUR

Wednesday: John 3:17

For God sent his Son into the world not to condemn the world, but so that through him the world might be saved.

Just like the crucifixion, so too the incarnation of Jesus is a clear sign of God's love. God does not love from a distance. As the Fourth Eucharistic prayer reminds us, "He became like us in all things but sin". In other words, the Son of God does not stand apart; he gets involved and meets us where we are. Our world is His world. His solidarity with us is wonderful to relate but we must always remember it is only half of the story. God became human so that all humanity could be saved, all humanity could become "God-like". We live in a world that looks everywhere and nowhere for solutions to its problems. It spends millions trying to save itself, but even today we need to remember that God still takes the initiative. Very soon, on Holy Saturday, many people in our parishes will respond to Christ's invitation to become part of his body, the Church. Their baptism and the renewal of our baptismal promises will be a timely reminder that salvation is God's gift and it is freely given.

For your daily reflection

✦ When Jesus was born he chose our common humanity. Picture in your mind a meeting with the Christ who walked about Palestine. What would it feel like to talk to and listen to the Son of God?

By the mystery of this water and wine may we come to share in the divinity of Christ who humbled himself to share in our humanity.
Prayer from the Liturgy of the Eucharist

People of God and Lay Formation
WEEK FOUR

Thursday: John 3.19

sentence is pronounced that the light has come into the world

John speaks of judgement in a particular way. For him, it is never God who judges humankind but humanity, by its choices, who judges itself. Using the symbol of light, Jesus says that people have a choice. Either they walk in the light or they choose darkness. On Holy Saturday, in the Solemn Vigil the Easter Candle is lit and these words are said: May the Light of Christ rising in glory dispel the darkness of our hearts and minds. At one and the same time the world can be anxious and frightened of, as well as oblivious to, the darkness in which it lives – fearful of the call to holiness. It is so easy for us to be influenced by this "darkness" rather than to be influential witnesses of the "light". So often we live as though darkness was stronger than light but, as the saying goes, it is always better to light a candle than curse the darkness. When we doubt this, we need to remember that God's judgement is that light scatters darkness; that goodness will *always* overcome evil.

For your daily reflection

✦ Do I believe that goodness is more powerful than evil?
✦ Asked by a stranger, what reasons could I give for the hope that is in me?

God of unchanging power and light,
  look with mercy and favour on your entire Church.
Bring lasting salvation to mankind,
  so that the world may see the fallen lifted up,
  the old made new,
  and all things brought to perfection,
  through him who is their origin,
  our Lord Jesus Christ,
  who lives and reigns for ever and ever.
Amen.

Prayer from the Easter Vigil (after the Seventh Reading)

People of God and Lay Formation
WEEK FOUR

Friday: John 3:21

but the man who lives by the truth comes out into the light

God wills everyone to live in the light of his love but so often we choose to live in darkness. So often, and for some reason, our eyes do not see the beauty of God's truth. Then the truth dawns and it is a fatal attraction! The lovely words of St Augustine of Hippo speak for the person who discovers this truth – "late have I loved you O Beauty so ancient and so new". The light is attractive – we are drawn to it. The light is beautiful and we bathe in its glow. The beauty of God is that he shows us how to live as truthful people. The people of God are meant to be a beautiful and attractive people. Their beauty, their love of God's truth should be so appealing that those around might "see the light!"

For your daily reflection

✦ Blessed Mother Theresa said, "Do something beautiful for God". How is my practice of Christianity beautiful and attractive to others?
✦ Am I aware that living in the light is good for me and beautiful to others?

"Walk as children of light ... and try to learn what is pleasing to the Lord.
Take no part in the unfruitful works of darkness" (Eph 5:8, 10-11).
Lord that I may see!
Evangelium Vitae 95, John Paul II, 1995

People of God and Lay Formation
WEEK FOUR

Saturday: John 3:21

so that it may be plainly seen that what he does is done in God

Wrought iron is metal that has been fashioned by its maker. Christians should be those people of whom it can be clearly seen that they have been moulded by God. The word church comes from a Greek word *Ek-klesia*. This word literally means "the called out people". A people who have not chosen one another but have been chosen by God. A people not simply chosen but moulded and fashioned. In other words 'wrought in God'. As St Peter would tell us, God has made the whole people of God: a chosen race, a royal priesthood, a holy nation, a people set apart. They are his witnesses; and because you are part of the Holy People you are his witness too. Daunted? – don't be. God never calls without providing you with all that you will need to be his witness – a living mystery of the God who so loved the world.

For your daily reflection

◆ Do I really believe that I was chosen and fashioned by God?
◆ If I were arrested for being a Christian, what evidence would there be to condemn me?

Through his cross and resurrection, he freed us from sin and death and called us to the glory that has made us a chosen race, a royal priesthood, a holy nation, a people set apart. Everywhere we proclaim your mighty works for you have called us out of darkness into your own wonderful light.
Preface of Sundays in Ordinary Time 1

People of God and Lay Formation
WEEK FOUR   GROUP SESSION

Opening Prayer

Lord God,
In love you have created us
and in your mercy redeemed us.
Fill us with your holy light
so that our lives may reflect
your love in the world.
We make this prayer through Jesus Christ
our Lord.
Amen.

Listen to the Bishop's teaching for this week by watching the DVD or by reading the extract below.

We are part of a society that has lost touch with its religious narrative, and lost confidence in its traditions of faith. We are an indifferent society more than a hostile one. If we are to witness to Christ and his resurrection, we need to be deeply grounded in our life of faith. In order to evangelise we ourselves must be evangelised. This is the *new evangelisation* that the Church in its teaching repeatedly calls us all to. If we are to speak about God we must have a renewed contact with God and his loving call to justice and mercy.

Extract from the Bishop's teaching

Reflecting on our Experience

- Have I ever seen myself as someone who evangelises?
- What, if anything, has helped me grow in my faith?

Explore the Scriptures

John 3:14-21

Jesus said to Nicodemus:

'The Son of Man must be lifted up as Moses lifted up the serpent in the desert, so that everyone who believes may have eternal life in him.
Yes, God loved the world so much that he gave his only Son, so that everyone who believes in him may not be lost but may have eternal life.
For God sent his Son into the world not to condemn the world, but so that through him the world might be saved.
No one who believes in him will be condemned; but whoever refuses to believe is condemned already, because he has refused to believe in the name of God's only Son.

People of God and Lay Formation
GROUP SESSION — WEEK FOUR

On these grounds is sentence pronounced: that though the light has come into the world men have shown they prefer darkness to the light because their deeds were evil.
And indeed, everybody who does wrong hates the light and avoids it, for fear his actions should be exposed; but the man who lives by the truth comes out into the light, so that it may be plainly seen that what he does is done in God.'

'God so loved the world' is a phrase we might know well but as Lent continues it is phrase that we need to know not simply in our heads but also deep in our hearts. It is a phrase to ponder and marvel at. God loves us for no other reason than he loves us. If you were the only person in the world – God would still have sent his Son for you. As individuals and as Church, we have been chosen in love. We become God's people not through any particular quality we possess but simply because God loves us. Our Diocese is a fascinating place not least because we are blessed with so many nations and cultures bringing life and vitality to our local church. Someone described us as the 'Church of all Nations'. In this multi-cultural Diocese, we have the great joy of experiencing that God's love is for all – he has no favourites. God so loved the whole world.

But his love demands a response from us. Why did God call us out, bring us to baptism, and make us into a holy people, a chosen nation, a people set apart? The document *Lumen Gentium* tells us why in such a simple and profound way: to bring the Light of Christ to the world. Each Easter we see how God, through baptism, brings new individuals to become part of the whole People of God. This Easter once again we shall see how so many of our new brothers and sisters have made the decision to choose the light. The light and the truth of Christ has attracted them because they have discovered what we already know: Christ's truth is beautiful and all his ways are good.

And yet our Gospel doesn't end there. Christ who attracted us also has more to do with us. God in Christ is wanting to fashion us so that the people of the world might be attracted by the witness of our lives, by the way we live. Through us people will be drawn to Christ who is Light because they will recognise that our lives are not of our own making. God has fashioned us – he has wrought his good work in us. Lent is always a reminder of the need to be refashioned in the image of Christ. This year our Diocese asks us to consider this challenge not only in Lent but throughout the

People of God and Lay Formation
WEEK FOUR GROUP SESSION

year and beyond. Adult faith formation, training for leadership and ministry will become opportunities for everyone in the Diocese. It is one of the ways that we can be re-formed so that the world can *clearly see* that the Church, the whole People of God, are there to bring light into the darkness of the modern world.

Reflect

✦ Share something that strikes you from the Gospel reading.
✦ Do I feel loved by God, deeply, personally?
✦ What steps must I take to accept the challenge of Christ to be refashioned in God's love? How do I need to be formed in faith?

Respond

✦ Find out if there are people in your parish being prepared for baptism and reception into the Church. What role can you play, as an individual and as a group, to welcome and support new members into your community?
✦ How can you help create or develop a climate of evangelisation and formation in your parish?

Contact details for help in the Diocese:
Parish Catechetical Support Team
(020 8202 3611)
www.rcdow.org.uk/education,

Diocesan Department of Pastoral Affairs
(020 7798 9363)
www.wdpastoral.co.uk

Closing Prayer

God our Father,
Let the Spirit you sent on your Church
to begin the teaching of the Gospel
continue to work in the world
through the hearts of all who believe.
We ask this through Christ our Lord.
Amen.

Opening prayer, Pentecost Sunday.

Working Together in Mission
WEEK FIVE

Our Bishop teaches

To make the Church the home and the school of communion: that is the great challenge facing us in the millennium which is now beginning, if we wish to be faithful to God's plan and respond to the world's deepest yearnings.
　　　　　　　　　　Novo Millennio Ineunte, no. 43

For the Church to be a *home and school of communion,* we must take on a spirituality of communion which will manifest itself in action, improved participation and collaboration and which is reflective of the diversity of roles and people in the Diocese of Westminster. Furthermore, a developed spirituality of communion is required in order to invigorate our structures. New ways and changed situations are unavoidable, but are not to be feared. Always and everywhere, the challenge of the Gospel is to be a people of hope, a hope that enriches and enables.

It is Jesus himself who says to those who follow him, "Do not be afraid." It was Cardinal Newman who reminded us that "To live is to change, and to be perfect is to have changed often." We will proceed in a climate of hope, enabling and enriching the vocation of each one of us.

At the conclusion of the White Paper, driven by the call in *Novo Millennio Ineunte,* I emphasise that mission and communion are at the heart of our spiritual and pastoral progress. We need to be in communion with each other in the Spirit of Christ. It is this living in communion that empowers us for the task of evangelisation to witness to Christ in word and deed.

The teaching of Pope John Paul II and now, Pope Benedict XVI, emphasises that active responsibility in the Church's life is for all – laity as well as clergy. It is time for a new *climate of listening* leading to a deeper understanding of one another – bishops, priests, people. All ministries together, united and collaborating, will sustain the community in all its many needs.

Working Together in Mission
WEEK FIVE

Fifth Sunday of Lent (2nd April)
John 12:20-30

Among those who went up to worship at the festival were some Greeks.
These approached Philip, who came from Bethsaida in Galilee, and put this request to him, 'Sir, we should like to see Jesus'.
Philip went to tell Andrew, and Andrew and Philip together went to tell Jesus.
Jesus replied to them: 'Now the hour has come for the Son of Man to be glorified.
I tell you, most solemnly, unless a wheat grain falls on the ground and dies, it remains only a single grain; but if it dies, it yields a rich harvest.
Anyone who loves his life loses it; anyone who hates his life in this world will keep it for the eternal life.
If a man serves me, he must follow me, wherever I am, my servant will be there too.
If anyone serves me, my Father will honour him. Now my soul is troubled. What shall I say: Father, save me from this hour?
But it was for this very reason that I have come to this hour.
Father, glorify your name!'
A voice came from heaven, 'I have glorified it, and I will glorify it again.'
People standing by, who heard this, said it was a clap of thunder; others said, 'It was an angel speaking to him'.
Jesus answered, 'It was not for my sake that this voice came, but for yours.
'Now sentence is being passed on this world; now the prince of this world is to be overthrown. And when I am lifted up from the earth, I shall draw all men to myself.'
By these words he indicated the kind of death he would die.

For your daily reflection

✦ The people said they would like to see Jesus. What is it that I wish to see or to understand?

Heavenly Father, send your Holy Spirit to empower us with courage and hope, that we may know with joy the path you have chosen for us.
Amen.

Working Together in Mission
WEEK FIVE

Monday: John 12:21

Sir, we should like to see Jesus

The Greeks were seeking a flesh and blood man, Jesus. People are still seeking him. Today he makes his presence known in us and through us in the minute details of our lives with others and through his whole body the Church. When we love, then he is visible, then he can be seen.

There are people around us who, if asked, we could point to and say: I know Jesus is alive because I have seen his face in the love shown by this person, by this act of generosity or welcome or compassion. Jesus is here, available to those asking for him, but quite often we fail to remember that it is we, here and now, who are called in our treatment of those around us to show Christ's presence to the world. Moreover, we know too that his life is often obscured by ours, his love covered over by our worries or tensions, his life eroded by our impatience, selfishness and preoccupation, by the reality of sin. Happy Lent then that we can recognise the poverty of our loving and ask for his forgiveness and healing.

For your daily reflection

✦ What is it that I need to be rid of for Christ's presence in me to be more obvious to others?

Heavenly Father,
Grant me the grace to live in your strength alone and to reveal the face of Christ to our seeking world.
Amen.

Working Together in Mission
WEEK FIVE

Tuesday: John 12:22

Philip went to tell Andrew, and Andrew and Philip together went to tell Jesus.

Jesus may well reveal himself directly, but more often than not Christ reveals himself to us through the actions, words and presence of others. Responding to the request "We want to see Jesus" Philip goes to Andrew for assistance and then, having drawn together, they move quite literally towards Christ. There is something about the nature of our working together as Christ's disciples, which will always lead us to him. Two thousand years ago Jesus chose particular men and women to witness to him and draw others to him. Today, no less than then, he chooses each one of us to be no less witnesses to his presence and love.

For your daily reflection

◆ Am I willing to pray and work with others in building up the community?

Heavenly Father,
Open our hearts and minds to your will and
grant us the grace of working together,
that others, by our words and actions,
may come to know the loving presence
of your Son, Jesus Christ.
Amen.

Working Together in Mission
WEEK FIVE

Wednesday: John 12:23-24

Jesus replied to them:
'Now the hour has come for the Son of Man to be glorified. I tell you, most solemnly,
unless a wheat grain falls on the ground and dies, it remains only a single grain;
but if it dies, it yields a rich harvest.

Explaining how the seed dies, Jesus points to the purpose of his existence – a self-sacrifice that is to bear fruit in the gift of eternal life. Jesus is urgently, pointedly, revealing the reality of the hour. This hour is upon us too, we have a mission to fulfil and we are called to respond to the unfolding story of his suffering and death; to die to the attitudes and behaviours that prevent the fruit from developing in our own lives and in the life of the Church. For the future growth of the Body of Christ, we need to look afresh at our faith and how we live it day to day in our parishes, homes and workplaces.

For your daily reflection

✦ Am I concerned about those who have yet to hear the Good News?
✦ What is the fruit of my daily labour? What is the fruit of my witnessing to the truth of God's loving forgiveness?

Loving Father,
Instill in us the courage to risk everything for you; that imitating Christ's confident trust we may put to death all that prevents us from obeying your will.
Amen.

Working Together in Mission
WEEK FIVE

rsday: John 12:25

Anyone who loves his life loses it; anyone who hates his life in this world will keep it for the eternal life.

Jesus uses radical ideas to stir us out of our complacency and to make us listen. What does this really mean? A simple illustration may help: Spider monkeys are attracted to shiny items and they are caught by a very simple method. Attractive jewellery is dropped into a tethered narrow-necked jar, in plain sight of the monkey. The monkey makes a grab at the jewellery as soon as the catcher moves away, but he can't withdraw his clenched fist from the jar, without letting go of the jewellery. Faced with his liberty or relinquishing the prize, the monkey chooses what he has in his hand and is captured. We too can be captured by the things of this world, affording our goods, our time and our space, an importance they do not deserve.

St Paul in his letters illustrates true freedom in Christ; happiness whether imprisoned or free, in want or well fed, in sickness or health. What we are offered through the love of Christ is a treasure far greater than anything this world can give – authentic freedom, being loved forever. We are called to see this freedom as a gift to be embraced by unclenching our fists and letting go of whatever we know destroys our responsiveness to God and to each other.

For your daily reflection

♦ To what extent do the things I own or value possess me?

Lord Jesus,
Implant is us an understanding of your complete and unconditional love, a love that encompasses all our needs, and which will grant us more than we can ask for or imagine.
Amen.

Working Together in Mission
WEEK FIVE

Friday: John 12:26

*If a man serves me, he must follow me, wherever I am, my servant will be there too.
If anyone serves me, my Father will honour him.*

Jesus' disciples physically followed him – walking, talking, eating, laughing. They saw him heal and weep and get angry in the temple. Empowered by the Holy Spirit they followed him living lives of service to the kingdom; loving witness, courageous proclamation, persecution, martyrdom. Having been rescued from their own weakness and cowardice, they were able to follow Christ. We know Christ today because of their faithful discipleship, because they passed on to others what they knew and how they loved. Our lives must give witness to those who will follow us. From the one to whom much is given, much is expected. There is no escape, yet we are not alone. Together we must share joyfully "passing on faith to new generations: and… building a Christian culture ready to evangelise the larger culture in which we live." (*Ecclesia in Europa propositio 8.2*)

For your daily reflection

✦ Are there places Jesus needs *me* to be and I am reluctant to go?
✦ When I recognise a need am I ready to ask the Holy Spirit to help me do what is needed even if it appears beyond me?

*Almighty Father,
You empowered the Apostles through the gift of your Holy Spirit. Empower and sustain us through the gift of that same Spirit, that our serving and following may spring from grateful and radiant hearts.
Amen.*

Working Together in Mission
WEEK FIVE

Saturday: John 12:27-28

Now my soul is troubled.
What shall I say: Father, save me from this hour?
But it was for this very reason
that I have come to this hour.
Father, glorify your name!'
A voice came from heaven, 'I have glorified it, and
I will glorify it again.'

We should take comfort that in his humanity Jesus knew what it was to have his soul troubled, what it was to wish that things could be other than they were. He truly knew our state, lived in it and died in it. We have no need to be afraid. That there is no need to fear is affirmed every time we celebrate the Eucharist. Here, just as the Father affirmed Christ by his presence and by his speaking, Christ affirms us, feeding us with his body and blood. Together we are fed on the Eucharist that enables us to live the resurrected lives we are called to live. This is the key to our hope and to the confident building up of our communities.

We are not expected to fulfil the mission of Christ in isolation. We are called to fulfil it strengthened by him. And strengthened by him to fulfil it in the very human connectedness and communion that is possible between us.

For your daily reflection

◆ What practical steps can I take today to affirm others in their witnessing to Christ and to call forth the resurrected life of Christ in them?

Mystery of mysteries this privilege that was given to us, this incredible, exorbitant, privilege.
To keep alive the words of life, to nourish with our blood, with our flesh, with our heart the words which, without us, would collapse fleshless.

Charles Péguy,
The Mystery of the Charity of Joan of Arc.

Working Together in Mission
WEEK FIVE   GROUP SESSION

Opening Prayer

Lord, help us to do your will that your Church may grow and become faithful in your service. Amen.
*   Opening prayer Tuesday, Fifth Week of Lent*

Listen to the Bishop's teaching for this week by watching the DVD or by reading the extract below.

For the Church to be a *home and school of communion,* we must take on a spirituality of communion which will manifest itself in action, improved participation and collaboration and which is reflective of the diversity of roles and people in the Diocese of Westminster. Furthermore, a developed spirituality of communion is required in order to invigorate our structures. New ways and changed situations are unavoidable, but are not to be feared. Always and everywhere, the challenge of the Gospel is to be a people of hope, a hope that enriches and enables.

*   Extract from the Bishop's teaching*

Reflecting on our Experience

- ✦ Collaboration involves challenge. Working in collaboration with anyone requires an understanding of them. Whose role and vocation do I need to understand more fully?
- ✦ The Church calls the baptised to the exercise of their common priesthood in serving each other and the world at large. What does this mean to me?

Explore the Scriptures

John 12:20-30

Among those who went up to worship at the festival were some Greeks.
These approached Philip, who came from Bethsaida in Galilee, and put this request to him, 'Sir, we should like to see Jesus'.
Philip went to tell Andrew, and Andrew and Philip together went to tell Jesus.
Jesus replied to them: 'Now the hour has come for the Son of Man to be glorified.
I tell you, most solemnly, unless a wheat grain falls on the ground and dies, it remains only a single grain; but if it dies, it yields a rich harvest.
Anyone who loves his life loses it; anyone who hates his life in this world will keep it for the eternal life.

GROUP SESSION — WEEK FIVE
Working Together in Mission

If a man serves me, he must follow me, wherever I am, my servant will be there too.
If anyone serves me, my Father will honour him.
Now my soul is troubled. What shall I say: Father, save me from this hour?
But it was for this very reason that I have come to this hour.
Father, glorify your name!'
A voice came from heaven,
'I have glorified it, and I will glorify it again.'
People standing by, who heard this,
said it was a clap of thunder; others said,
'It was an angel speaking to him'.
Jesus answered, 'It was not for my sake that this voice came, but for yours.
'Now sentence is being passed on this world; now the prince of this world is to be overthrown.
And when I am lifted up from the earth,
I shall draw all men to myself.'
By these words he indicated the kind of death he would die.

This Gospel passage takes us on a journey of faith. We meet a faithful people travelling to the great festival by following in the footsteps of generations who have gone before them. At their journeys' end they experience the reality of Jesus' presence in the holy city. This is true for us who follow in the footsteps of our great tradition who are part of the continuous community of faith called the Church. People sought Jesus and they were led to find him through the actions of the disciples. Our actions count, our responses to conversations matter. Jesus taught them about the purpose of his life, of the seed dying and fruit being created. Jesus makes it clear that our way is to follow Him, to become of service to him, with our actions proclaiming, enacting and inspiring others to seek and follow him too.

The treasure we are promised, the glorifying of God, means that we do not have to be afraid to be generous. We can serve God fully, in the knowledge that in his love, nothing is wasted; that even if our efforts seem unappreciated or unrewarded, he knows our hearts and will bring forth fruits from our faithfulness in his due season.

What confidence we can have therefore as we work together; lay people, priests, religious and bishops. We are truly one family, united forever in Christ's body. We have only to believe it and learn how to live that unity with each other. What seems impossible with our human resources, can be met in full with the power of the Holy Spirit living in us. We can co-operate across parish boundaries, we can work alongside those we have not met before, we can rejoice in the connectedness of our lives, we can generously listen to each other and make plans for the future. All this is possible, even as we move forward into uncertain times of change. We can be confident always, because it is Christ himself who leads us, feeds us and calls us to work beside him for the world that is hungering for his love.

Let us ask for the power and faith to work towards a vibrant church community.

Reflect

- Share something that strikes you from the Gospel reading.
- If we believe the above is true, that working together can be more productive, what practical steps must we take to reap this new fruit?
- What do we see as our role in the unfolding developments in our Diocese? Are we willing to participate in future developments?

Respond

- Just as we have been told to unite with other Christians and to do what is possible together, even more should we apply this to our own parishes. So, let us find ways to join hands across parish boundaries and actively seek to support one another.
- What opportunities can you see for greater collaboration in the life of your parish, with other parishes and within the deanery and the Diocese as a whole?

To conclude our Lenten reflections, watch the Cardinal's 'Holy Week and Final Prayer' on the DVD or read the Cardinal's prayer together.

Closing Prayer

Heavenly Father,
we thank you for all your goodness to us
and we ask you to help us
here in our Diocese of Westminster
to continue to deepen our faith and hope
and love of your Son Jesus Christ
so that we may show him to others
by the way we live
and give glory to you, our Father.
We ask this through the same Jesus Christ,
our Lord.
Amen.

Cardinal Cormac Murphy-O'Connor

Meditations for Palm Sunday and Holy Week

HOLY WEEK

Palm Sunday (9th April)
Mark 15:39

Truly this man was the Son of God

The Centurion echoes the words that had opened the Gospel of Mark, "The beginning of the Good News of Jesus Christ the Son of God". As we begin Holy Week, we read the Passion of Our Lord and we know that Jesus will suffer terribly and be put to death in a most horrible way. In any circumstances, such suffering and injustice is unacceptable, but we must remember throughout the events of this week that the victim is none other than the Son of God himself. And why did God allow all this to happen? All these events speak of just one reason – God loved the world so much that he sent his Son to be our redeemer. All the events that we commemorate this week show God's determination to love us and, despite ourselves and all our failings, to save us for eternal life.

For your daily reflection

✦ How have I shown my love for Christ by loving others until it hurts?

Father, in these days of Holy Week, may we walk with Jesus through his rejection and suffering so that we may then celebrate the wonderful truth of his Resurrection. Amen.

Monday of Holy Week
John 12:10-11

And the chief priests plotted to kill Lazarus too, because many of the Jews were turning away and believing in Jesus because of him.

Here is the final reminder before the passion of the Lord, that Jesus did not walk alone in his ministry. It was often through the testimony of others that Jesus became known. Lazarus had been raised by Jesus from the dead and people believed in Jesus because they saw Lazarus alive. Every Christian is invited to bring people to faith in Christ, to be silent witnesses to him by their lives and actions. We are part of Holy Week because we are walking with the Lord – he invites us to stay close to him, first through his suffering, so that we may share in his glory.

For your daily reflection

✦ How might I go about inviting someone to faith in Christ?

Father, in these holiest days of the Church's year may we come to a new understanding of our faith, and give our belief full expression in our lives. Amen.

Meditations for Palm Sunday and Holy Week

HOLY WEEK

Tuesday of Holy Week
John 13:30

And it was night.

All goodness seems to be evaporating. The opposition is growing and the followers of Jesus are still unaware of the dangers. One of them will betray Jesus to the authorities. All the rest will run away, frightened. The ministry of Christ has come to an end in seeming disaster. And it was night. But with all the fear that comes with night and darkness, there remains always the promise of a new dawn and the beginning of a new day. After the darkness and despair of the passion will come the Resurrection and the invitation to new life.

For your daily reflection

✦ Where and in what situations am I called to be a messenger of hope?

Father, as we contemplate the death of your Son may it deepen our desire for new life and new possibilities by the power of his Resurrection. Amen.

Wednesday of Holy Week
John 13:21-22

"Amen, I say to you, one of you will betray me". Deeply distressed at this, they began to say to him one after another,
"Surely it is not I, Lord?"

We can imagine the distress of the disciples. They had followed the Lord for some three years and he had been their leader, guide, mentor and friend. Confused by things he taught and the real meaning of the things that he did, they still knew that it was right to follow him and believe in him. They could not believe that they could betray him. But they all ran away at the time of the arrest. We run away, too, when we fail to witness to our faith or fail to recognise an opportunity to love others in his name. We fail him, too, when we do not make him known. Betray you, Lord? Surely not me. . . .

For your daily reflection

✦ When have I betrayed you Lord?
✦ In the garden Jesus asked his disciples to stay nearby to watch and pray. How can I give myself fully to the Lord during the Easter Triduum over the next three days? Can I find an opportunity to spend time with the Lord?

Father, for your endless willingness to forgive and for the grace to turn even my mistakes to the good, I thank you. Amen.